tips and tidbits

for the

horse lover

By Tena Bastian

with illustrations by Tami Zigo

BICENTENNIAL
1807
WILEY
2007
BICENTENNIAL

Wiley Publishing, Inc.

Howell Book House
Published by Wiley Publishing, Inc., Hoboken, New Jersey

For general information on our other products and services or to obtain technical support please contact our Customer Care Department within the U.S. at (800) 762-2974, outside the U.S. at (317) 572-3993 or fax (317) 572-4002.

Wiley also publishes its books in a variety of electronic formats. Some content that appears in print may not be available in electronic books. For more information about Wiley products, please visit our web site at www.wiley.com.

Library of Congress Cataloging-in-Publication Data:
Bastian, Tena.

Tips and tidbits for the horse lover / by Tena Bastian ; with illustrations by Tami Zigo.

p. cm.

ISBN-13: 978-0-470-17126-4 (cloth)

ISBN-10: 0-470-17126-X

1. Horsemanship--Miscellanea. 2. Horses--Miscellanea. I. Title.

SF285.B335 2008

636.1--dc22

2007017907

Printed in China

10 9 8 7 6 5 4 3 2 1

Book design by Kathie S. Rickard
Wiley Bicentennial Logo: Richard J. Pacifico
Book production by Wiley Publishing, Inc. Composition Services

She literally took my breath away . . .

In Loving Memory

of

Rachel Lynn Shute

This book is dedicated to her spirit, her smile and her beautiful soul.
Heaven holds a place for her in a green pasture full of fast horses.
Love always finds a way to keep those we love close to us.
Whisper her name on a warm summer day and she will smile
and know you remember her.

—Tena

Table of Contents

If you find yourself either firmly entrenched in, or falling into the world of horses, welcome, come on in and get to know us all, you're in good company.

Horses have touched every corner of entertainment, from movies, to music, to literature.

History was built on the back of a horse. Take a stroll through the ages and see how horses have made their mark.

# acknowledgments

I would like to acknowledge the following individuals and groups for their continued support and contribution to this collection of Tips and Tidbits . . .

Courtney Doss and Wrangler Jeans Corporation

Dave Moore and Bari Frankel and Frye Boots

David Towle at Rio Vista Products

Pi Poletta at Tri-Tronics

Kate Epstein at Epstein Literary Agency

The Quarterhorse Group at Yahoogroups

Hollowbrook Farms

Laura and Jeff Stratton and the Murnan Road Posse

Equine Affaire

www.thestallionsource.com

Tami Zigo for her whimsical artwork

Roxane Cerda, Howell Book House and Wiley Publishing for their hard work

Dr. William "Billy" Bergin

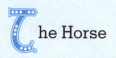 he Horse

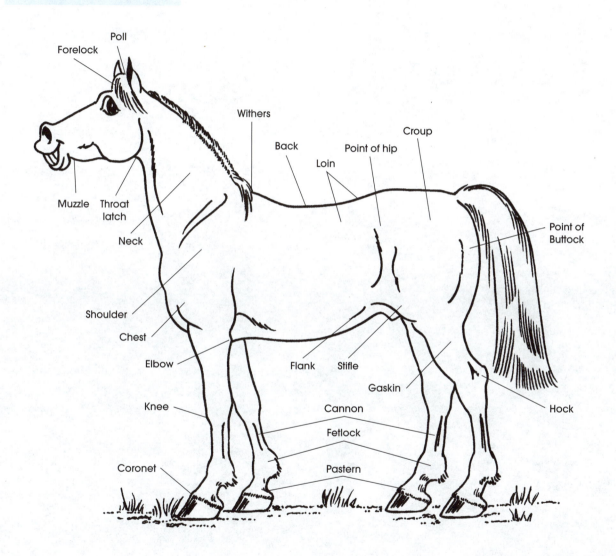

In good Company

The term "drop a stick" on a horse means to measure her height; that is, to see how tall she is. A horse's height is measured in *hands*, from the ground to her *withers*—the bone at the point where her mane ends and her back begins. Each hand equals four inches, originally based on the average width of a human hand. A horse that is said to be fifteen hands is actually sixty inches tall at the withers. If a horse measures more than an exact number of hands, the extra inches are shown after a decimal point, so a horse that is fifteen hands and three inches is written 15.3 hh. The tallest horse ever recorded is a Shire named Samson, who stood just over 21.2 hh. Keeping in mind that a hand is four inches, this horse stood over seven feet tall! The shortest horse in history was named Little Pumpkin, who stood a mere fourteen inches tall.

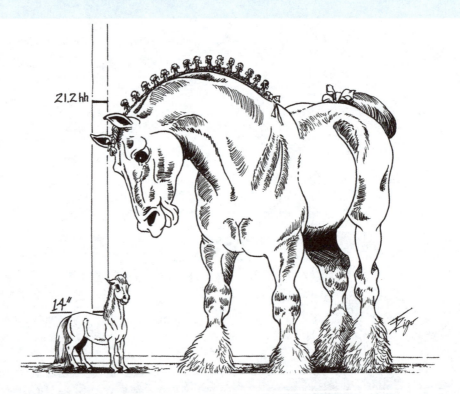

> " Training a horse is like an abbreviated process of raising a child. Fortunately it doesn't take as long to train a horse as it does to raise a child, but in the end, we want the same result for both – we want to see that child and that horse go out and do the best possible. "

—Richard Shrake, Resistance Free Training

Can't decide where to go for vacation? Make plans to attend one of the exciting and informative equine expos (or horse expos) across the country. These expos are your chance to learn from a variety of clinicians, all gathered together in one place. Search online or call your breed association for a schedule of events. And book your trip early, because hotels fill up quickly!

According to the American Horse Council, there are more than 9.2 million horses in the United States. Specifically, they are used for:

Recreation	42%
Showing	30%
Racing	9%
Other	19%

It is estimated that there are 256,000 horses in Colorado alone, which generate $956 million. That is quite a contribution to the national economy.

If you're a science buff, the scientific classification of the horse is as follows:

Kingdom: Animalia
Phylum: Chordata
Subphylum: Vertebrata
Class: Mammalia
Subclass: Theria
Infraclass: Eutheria
Order: Perissodactyla
Family: Equidae

Although only about 11 percent of the world's human population is left-handed, a horse is usually led and mounted from the left side.

The average horse's heart, considered the center of everything both physical and emotional, weighs approximately eight and a half to nine pounds.

The American Quarter Horse is appropriately named for its ability to run a quarter mile at high speed. The American Quarter Horse Association is the world's largest single breed equine association, with approximately 350,000 members and more than 4.5 million registered horses.

Winter weather not only makes a leather bridle brittle, it also makes a bit a bit too cold. (Try saying that three times quickly!) Keep your leather in excellent shape and offer your horse a nice, warm bit by bringing your bridle into the house with you at night, or by tucking it inside your winter coat while you groom and saddle your horse.

The most common facial markings on a horse are:

- ★ Star: A white patch on the forehead, usually between the eyes
- ★ Strip: A white patch that extends lengthwise down the face and is no wider than the nasal bones
- ★ Blaze: Wider than a strip, a white patch that covers the forehead and the front of the horse's face and extends down toward the mouth
- ★ Snip: A patch of white between the nostrils

Common leg color markings are:

- ★ Coronet: The hair just above the hoof is white
- ★ Pastern: A white band that includes the coronet and pastern
- ★ Sock: White hair that comes to just above the fetlock
- ★ Stockings: White hair that comes all the way up to just below the knee

Horses should have clean, fresh water available at all times. The rule of thumb is to ask yourself whether or not you would drink it. If the answer is no, it's definitely time to clean the water buckets.

"You are a great champion. When you ran, the ground shook. The sky opened and mere mortals parted. Parted the way to victory where you will meet me in the winner's circle. Where I will lay a blanket of flowers on your back."

—Dakota Fanning and Kris Kristofferson in *Dreamer*

If you opt to keep your horse in a stall, it's recommended that the stall be no smaller than 10 feet x 10 feet for an average size horse. She should be able to move and turn with ease. Ensure a safe environment by entering the stall periodically to check for protruding nails, holes in the wall, or broken boards. Keep the stall clean and dry and limit the time your horse spends inside. Nothing is better for your horse than fresh air and sunshine. On rainy days when your horse will be spending more time inside, keep a radio in the barn tuned to her favorite station, and be sure the barn is well ventilated.

China boasts the largest population of horses, estimated at over eight million.

I saw a child that couldn't walk, sit on a horse, laugh and talk . . . I saw a child who could only crawl, mount a horse and sit up tall. I saw a child born into strife, take up and hold the reins of life. And that same child was heard to say, thank God for showing me the way.

—John Anthony Davis

New Year's Day is not only the first day of the year; it's the day that all registered horses turn one year older. Happy Birthday to the horse!

According to the American Horse Council, approximately one out of every sixty-three Americans is involved in horses to some extent. This means that 4.6 million Americans are involved in the equine industry in some way. Are you one of them?

One of the biggest misconceptions among newcomers to the horse world is that a pony is a young horse. This is not true. The term *foal* is used to describe a young horse. Ponies are a classification of equine breeds that are generally shorter than breeds considered horses. While not a hard and fast rule, it is usually true that breeds fourteen-and-a-half hands and under are considered ponies, and larger breeds are generally referred to as horses.

There are approximately 75 million horses in the entire world, and no two are exactly alike. That makes them sort of like snowflakes, doesn't it?

Unlike human teeth, horses' teeth continue to grow throughout their lives. The diet of a modern-day horse may not provide enough grit to keep the teeth worn down to a normal level, which can lead to many problems if left unchecked. Your horse's teeth should be floated (filed) once a year.

There are twelve animals that represent the Chinese New Year, and the horse is one of those twelve animals. This means that every twelve years truly is the year of the horse.

In order for a horse to learn, she must be relaxed, calm, and focused. Horses have excellent memories, and if you teach a horse through trust and patience, she can learn a great deal. If taught with force and fear, the only thing she will learn is to despise you.

Afraid you may not be able to afford a horse? Some figures from the American Horse Council should help you decide. Approximately 46 percent of horse owners have an income between $25,000 and $75,000, and only 28 percent have an income over $100,000.

There are more than 350 breeds of horses and ponies.

Here is a little rhyme to remind you of some of the more basic color possibilities of a horse.

Black, brown, bay

Sorrel, chestnut, grey

Buckskin, dun, paint, or pinto

Appaloosa, Palomino

These are the basic colors that go

With almost every horse I know.

On the back of the fetlock joint is a small horny growth called an *ergot*. It is believed to be a lingering remnant of the prehistoric horse. Depending on the horse, the ergot can be barely noticeable or may grow long enough that you may want to ask your farrier to trim it.

Before heading to Alabama, you should probably know that it is illegal to wrestle bears, to play dominoes on Sunday, to wear a mask in public, and to open an umbrella on the street for fear of spooking horses.

For a hoof injury, a disposable diaper secured with duct tape makes an excellent alternative to expensive packing and bandaging.

> If you have it, it is for life. It is a disease for which there is no cure. You will go on riding even after they have to haul you on to a comfortable wise old cob, with feet like inverted buckets and a back like a fireside chair.

—Monica Dickens, *Talking of Horses*

It has been said that, "You can lead a horse to water but you can't make him drink." You can, however, encourage him to drink by flavoring the water with apple juice or a flavored sports drink.

If you encounter a horse with a red ribbon tied in his tail, this is usually a sign that she is known to kick.

Did you know that a red horse is referred to as a sorrel?

 To come face to face with my fantasy, to once again feel whole. To look into your eyes and realize the depth of my own soul.

—The author, from her poem "Iron Horse"

In parts of Indiana, think twice before you give a cigarette to a monkey, sell a car on Sunday, catch a fish with your bare hands, and most importantly, before you pass a horse on the street. All of these acts could land you in jail—well, technically anyway.

There are horses living in every state in the nation, 45 of which have at least 20,000 horses each.

Horses are herbivores, which means that they primarily consume plant material. While they may consume some insects or even small rodents while grazing, plants meet almost all their nutritional needs. Horses have small stomachs, so they cannot digest large amounts of food at one time. Horses should be fed small amounts at a time, and feeding times should be spread over a period of ten to twelve hours.

An excellent winter treat for your horse is to mix up a batch of oatmeal and add some applesauce and a little cinnamon. It contains everything that your horse loves and warms them from the inside out.

According to the American Horse Council, a whopping 2 million people own horses and the industry as a whole pays the government an estimated $1.9 billion in taxes each year.

Old Billy, who lived to be 62 years old, is the oldest recorded horse. Born in England, this draft horse lived from 1760 to 1822.

When barbed wire was patented back in 1874, it was appropriately referred to as *the devil's rope*, due to the damage it could cause to horses and livestock. Yet even now, barbed wire is still in common use in the United States.

Every year in October, Quarter Horse enthusiasts gather in Columbus, Ohio, for the world's largest single breed horse show. The All American Quarter Horse Congress is a three-week event that attracts more than 650,000 attendees, exhibitors, and merchants from all over the world.

A horse who is well cared for should live well into her mid to late twenties. A horse's advanced age becomes apparent by characteristics such as a sway back, a loss of teeth, and a thinning of the body.

Miniature horses are now being trained and used as assistance animals. The prototype for such useful animals is said to have been a mini by the name of Twinkie.

A horse is considered an adult at just 4 years of age. A horse's father is referred to as his *sire*, while his mother is called his *dam*.

 If wishes were horses, then beggars would ride.

—Old Scottish Proverb

Horses have some unique jobs, and just one of those jobs is to help in physical therapy. The American Hippotherapy Association concludes that hippotherapy, the use of horses in physical therapy, has been shown to improve muscle tone, balance, posture, coordination, motor development, and emotional well-being in people with disabilities.

Thrush is an anaerobic bacterial disease of the horse's hoof, easily diagnosed by the presence of a distinct foul odor in the hoof. Keeping your horse's hooves clean and dry is the best prevention, but if your horse does develop thrush, consult your veterinarian for the best course of treatment.

Tens of millions of people attend horse-related events each year. If you're not yet one of them, you might consider finding a show near you.

Every horse has his or her own *sweet spot*, a particular spot where she likes to be scratched. Whether it is under the jaw line, on the chest, or up at the top of her tail, find your horse's sweet spot and scratch it now and then, and she will look forward to your coming to the barn.

When teaching a horse to lead beside you, never turn and look at the horse. Keep your eyes straight ahead and lean forward slightly. Your body language and slight pressure on the lead will encourage her to move forward.

The North American Riding for the Handicapped Association (NARHA) has more than 650 certified riding centers across the United States and Canada that offer more than 30,000 individuals therapy through the use of horses, proving once again that horses are good for the body and soul.

A horse who is younger than 3 years old has an attention span of about fifteen minutes, so keep your lessons short.

A *stallion* is a male horse who is capable of reproduction; a *gelding* is a male horse who has been altered so that he can no longer reproduce. A *mare* is a female horse. Stallions becomes sexually aware between 1 and 2 years of age, but most are not mentally mature enough for breeding until they are 3 to 5 years old. Of course, this depends on the individual stallion; like people, horses are individuals and mature at their own rates.

Horses are physically incapable of vomiting.

Horses are not predatory animals and are themselves prey animals. Their instinct tells them to flee from—rather than confront—danger.

If given free roaming pasture space, the average horse will graze for ten to fifteen hours each day. However, the types of grasses in any pasture vary greatly, and some plants and grasses can be toxic. For example, some fescue grasses can actually be quite dangerous to the pregnant mare, causing complications in pregnancy and delivery. It's important to know what's growing in your pasture and remove any toxic plants.

Colostrum is the first milk that a foal receives from her mother. It is extremely rich and contains the necessary antibodies and protein that a new foal requires. A young horse's first set of teeth are referred to as *milk teeth,* which are eventually replaced by permanent teeth between the ages of 3 and 5. Most horses have all of their adult teeth by the age of 5.

A baby horse is described as a *foal* for the first year of life. A *colt* is a boy, and a *filly* is a girl.

Now that's Entertainment

In the movie *Hidalgo*, as many as 550 horses were used in a scene. Trainer Rex Peterson supplied five American Paint Horses to play Hidalgo, and star Viggo Mortenson purchased one of his costars, RH Tecontender, "TJ."

In Washington Irving's *The Legend of Sleepy Hollow*, the horse ridden by Ichabod Crane was named Gunpowder, and Ichabod is described as a truly unskillful rider. In contrast, the antagonist, Brom, rides Daredevil, "a creature, like himself, full of mettle and mischief, and which no one but himself could manage."

In the 1938 movie, *The Adventures of Robin Hood,* Maid Marian, played by Oscar winner Olivia de Haviland, rides a beautiful palomino. Said to be the smartest horse in the movies, this well-known horse could, according to some, turn on a dime and give you nine cents change. He later went on to costar with another actor whose name may sound more familiar. That actor was none other than Roy Rogers, and you are probably familiar with the palomino by his stage name, Trigger.

In 2006, actress Whoopi Goldberg adopted a retired New York Police Department patrol horse after the horse was injured while on duty. This is rumored to be the second NYPD horse that the actress has adopted. Other celebrity horse lovers include Ellen DeGeneres, Darryl Hannah, Madonna, and William Shatner, just to name a few.

Fledge, the winged horse in C.S Lewis's *The Magician's Nephew*, was originally named Strawberry and pulled a hansom cab in London before being given wings and a new name.

In San Francisco, California, it is illegal to pile manure more than six feet high on any street corner.

Drawing crowds by the thousands, a potent attraction at the 1904 World's Fair was a horse by the name of Jim Key, dubbed "The Smartest Horse In The World." If you wonder who could possibly train a horse to read, write, spell, sort mail, tell time, and debate politics, it was none other than the self-taught veterinarian, former slave, and Civil War veteran Dr. William Key. Loved and admired by millions, and in my opinion one of the true horse communicators to this day, Dr. Key is considered to be an anti-cruelty pioneer.

> *Four things greater than all things are—*
> *Women and Horses and Power and War.*

—Rudyard Kipling, "The Ballad of the King's Jest"

More than 200 carriage horses clip-clop through the streets of New York City. According to the law, horses cannot be worked when the temperature rises over 90 degrees or drops below 18 degrees.

TV icon Mr. Ed began his life in El Monte, California, in 1949. His original name was Bamboo Harvester. He won four Patsy awards (animal Oscars) for his work and was quietly laid to rest at the age of 21.

The term *colic* refers to general pain in the horse's abdomen and is the number-one killer of horses. Signs of colic can include a lack of interest in feed, pawing the ground, biting or kicking at her sides, or rolling frequently and thrashing. Colic can have a number of causes and ranges from mild to severe. Helping your horse survive a bout with colic can depend on getting help quickly. The Colic and Digestive Disease Program of North Carolina State University's Equine Health Program conducts research targeting ways to better treat colic. They've created a helpful brochure outlining good emergency colic care. You can find it at http://www.cvm.ncsu.edu/docs/PDFS/colic_brochure.pdf. Download it before you need it, and keep it handy.

Did you know that in the video game series *Ultima*, Iolo's horse, Smith, actually talks and gives clues to the player?

Bing Crosby was partial owner of a ranch near San Diego, California, in 1932. The manager of the ranch was a breeder from Noblesville, Indiana, by the name of Roy Cloud. At the age of 3, one young foal from the ranch, Golden Cloud, was sold to Hudkins Stables—known for providing horses for movies. Throughout the estimated 80 films and 101 television episodes that followed, this horse never fell once. He was fast and steady and loved by millions. His face adorned everything from posters to lunchboxes and on July 3, 1965, at a ranch in Hidden Valley, California, Golden Cloud passed away at the age of 33. When his owner, who had once paid a mere $2,500 for this magnificent horse, mourned the loss of his friend, he was known by a more familiar name. The owner of this well-known and much-loved golden Palomino was Roy Rogers, and the horse was none other than the legendary Trigger.

" ... a lot of this is nuts and bolts stuff ... if the rider's nuts, the horse bolts. "

—Nicholas Evans, *The Horse Whisperer*

Cass Ole, the beautiful black Arabian stallion who portrayed the Black Stallion in the movie of the same name, actually had four white socks and a star. Cass Ole was a trained show horse, and producers and directors wanted so badly to use him for the part that they went to the trouble of dyeing his white socks and star black.

A healthy adult horse should have a heart rate of thirty to forty beats per minute while at rest. The respiratory rate of an adult horse should be approximately eight to twelve breaths per minute. Horses are incapable of breathing through their mouths, which is why they don't pant like a dog.

Horses have long been characterized in song, from "Wildfire" by Michael Martin Murphey and "The Old Grey Mare" to "A Horse with No Name" by America and "Chestnut Mare" by the Byrds.

In an attempt to catch a horse, never chase him. Instead, teach him to come to you. This may require a reward or incentive when the horse refuses to come to you at first; however, if you work on building trust long-term, you will have a friend you won't have to chase.

According to the American Horse Council, there are approximately 698,000 horses in California, over 70 percent of them involved in showing and recreational riding. What do you suppose the other 30 percent do all day?

Each July, in Chincoteague, Virginia, the Chincoteague Volunteer Fire Department holds a carnival, concert, and other weekend events to raise money for their department. All of these events are centered on Pony Penning, the annual roundup, pony swim, and auction of the wild ponies of Chincoteague Island by "saltwater cowboys." The time of the day of the round up depends on the tide: The ponies swim the narrowest part of the channel and always at low tide. The pony auction not only raises money for the fire department, it also helps them retain their grazing permit, which stipulates that the department must keep the herd down to 150 ponies or fewer. The classic book *Misty of Chincoteague* by Marguerite Henry depicts the story of one of the Chincoteague ponies.

Approximately 85 percent of a raw apple is comprised of water, making it an excellent treat for horses. Be sure to core the apple and slice it into pieces to prevent the horse from choking on the core. When feeding a horse a treat from your hand, do so from the outstretched palm of your hand. He cannot see what's in your hand and may mistake your fingers for the treat.

" The horse, the Horse! The symbol of surging potency and power of movement, of action, in man. "

—D.H. Lawrence, British author, *Apocalypse*, 1931

Tennessee is known for some excellent horses and country music, but it also has a few entertaining laws that are still on the books. It is illegal to lasso a fish, a person can still be hanged for stealing a horse, and in Knoxville, all businesses must have a hitching post.

The average mare is pregnant for 340 days. At the time of birth, the average foal weighs between 100 and 150 pounds. Within one hour, the foal should be standing and nursing.

Always look behind you before backing your horse. It is no different than driving a car; you should always know what is behind you.

In Florida, there are approximately 500,000 horses, producing horse industry goods and services worth $3 billion. By comparison, Indiana contributes a total of $779 million each year to the nationwide horse industry.

ollywood legend holds that Mr. Ed, from the famous television series, used to throw temper tantrums when he didn't get the "star" treatment.

Most horses that are thought to be white are actually not white at all. If you look closely, they have little black and white hairs dispersed throughout their coats, so they are considered gray instead.

When a horse points her nose to the sky and raises her upper lip, it is to better locate a smell. Horses have a very keen sense of smell and always stay very attuned to their surroundings. A stallion will do this when he senses a mare in season, and any horse may do this to locate a specific horse in a herd.

There were numerous horses featured in J.R.R. Tolkien's *The Lord of the Rings*. Of the most notable are Arod, Legolas' horse, little Bill the Pony, owned by the Hobbits, Sharp Ears, owned by Merry Brandybuck, Husufel and Brege, ridden by Aragorn, and Gandalf's horse Shadowfax.

Horses roll for a number of reasons. When a healthy horse rolls, it is a method of grooming to reach and scratch spots that can't be reached otherwise. In the summer, rolling also creates a barrier of dirt between a horse's skin and pesky bugs. In a herd of horses, lying down or rolling seems to be contagious. If one horse lies down or rolls, the others will follow because they know it is safe to do so.

In Laura Ingalls Wilder's treasured collection of *Little House* stories, the two horses owned by her family were named Sam and David, and the two wild colts owned by Almanzo Wilder, Laura's husband-to-be, were named Barnum and Skip.

A long whip is often used to guide a horse while longeing; however, the whip never actually touches the horse. Did you know that a whip makes a cracking sound due to the fact that the tip moves faster than the speed of sound?

Keeping records makes keeping horses much easier. Tracking things such as vet and farrier visits, shots and deworming schedules, and contact information for equine professionals and fellow horse lovers, in one place is helpful every day, but especially in the case of an emergency. You can purchase one of the various record keeping programs available at most tack stores, or create your own! You can also contact your local Pony Club or 4-H extension office and purchase project books for a few dollars each. They are full of useful information in an easy-to-understand format, and the equine record keeping project book is particularly useful.

In the *Valdemar* book series by Mercedes Lackey, "companions" are referred to as human spirits which are reincarnated in the form of white horses.

Never leave a halter on a horse when not using it to lead the horse. Not only is it easy for the horse to catch it on something and get injured, but as the horse grows, the halter will become too tight and irritate the skin. When teaching a horse to lead, apply light but constant pressure on the lead rope. Once the horse gives to the pressure and moves forward, release the pressure and praise him. When leading, never stand in front of the horse; it sends a mixed signal by creating a barrier in the direction that you wish him to move. Instead, stand next to the horse, facing forward.

In the famous television series *Mr. Ed*, Wilbur discovers that Ed can talk while brushing him for the first time. Although brushing your horse won't make him speak, it will make him extremely grateful. Not only does brushing a horse keep his coat clean and shiny, it also acts as a massage, stimulating muscles and relaxing both the horse and the groomer. Brushing is therapeutic and who knows, your horse just may thank you for it—literally!

According to an article in *The Gaited Horse*, Elvis Presley loved horses and owned several over the years. While in search of a golden Palomino, he got up at 3 a.m. to visit various farms and ranches to ask them if they had one for sale. He finally found one, purchased the horse, and named him Rising Sun. He then renamed his barn, House of the Rising Sun. Priscilla joked that Elvis purchased horses for his friends and bodyguards whether they wanted one or not!

Myths, Legends, and History

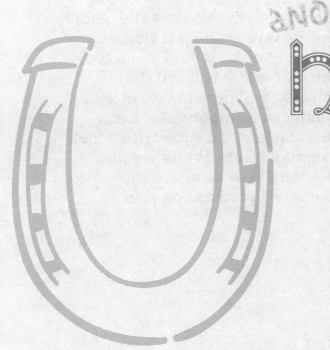

Horses have a strong sense of smell and the ability to remember people. Some Native American tribes used to blow gently into the face of a horse to introduce their scent for future recognition.

Some believe it to be an old wives' tale while others swear by it, but regardless of whether it works or not, it is interesting that paprika is said to darken the color of a Palomino's coat. Lore has it that paprika sprinkled on feed will darken the color by as much as three shades. It is important to know that paprika contains capsaicin, a substance which is banned in many equine sports. Whatever the reason, always check with your veterinarian before using any herbal or natural products on your horses.

While some behavior is genetic or hereditary, horses learn a lot of their behavior by example. A young horse will learn by imitating her mother or other horses in the herd almost from the moment she is born.

A chimeric (ky-mare-ik) horse, although extremely rare, is the result of an individual horse formed from two different cell lines. According to the American Quarter Horse Association, there are approximately fifteen chimeric horses out of their estimated 4.7 million registered horses! Oddly enough, scientists believe that these horses are the result of two non-identical twin embryos that somehow fuse into one embryo very early on in their development, thus giving them two sets of DNA. The trait is usually distinguishable by the color of the hair and skin. The coat takes on a rare brindle pattern with two different colors dispersed throughout. Chimerism has also been documented in cats and humans.

Before the invention of the automobile, horses played a huge part in people's everyday lives. Horses were used not only for recreation, but also for transportation and work. It's now estimated that there are more than 133 million cars being driven in the United States. If the automobile hadn't been invented, that would be a lot of horses running around.

When horses are excited, startled, or just out in the pasture at play, they will often lift their tails straight up in the air while they move around.

The colors of the horses ridden by the infamous Four Horsemen of the Apocalypse were symbolic. The first horse was white for conquest, the second red for war, followed by a black horse for famine, and finally a pale horse for death.

My beautiful, my beautiful! That standest meekly by,

With thy proudly-arched and glossy neck, and dark and fiery eye!

—Caroline Sheridan Norton, British poet, "The Arab's Farewell To His Steed"

Always end every lesson with your horse on a good note, regardless of how long it takes. Reward good behavior and understand that misbehavior, left unchecked, can quickly turn into a big problem. Notice it, address it, correct it, and move on.

Measuring about thirteen hands with short legs and a short neck, the Przewalski's horse is a small, stocky wild horse that once lived in Western Mongolia and Northern China. While they look similar to ponies, they have two more chromosomes than other horses. In Mongolia, they are called Takhi, which means spirit. According to the National Geographic Society, these horses are considered endangered, and it is estimated that there are approximately 1,200 of them living in zoos, private preserves, and protected areas of Mongolia.

The Tennessee Walking Horse used to be referred to as a *turn row* horse because of the breed's ability to turn sharply between rows of cotton.

Horses bond and form relationships through grooming each other. They will gently bite and rub on another horse much in the same way that a dog becomes familiar with another dog. You will often see a horse pulling on a fellow horse's halter in an effort to encourage her to play.

" Politicians are like the bones of a horse's fore shoulder — not a straight bone in it. **"**

Wendell Phillips, speech, July of 1864

The Pony Express, which utilized between 80 and 100 riders and approximately 400 horses, ran 1,966 miles from St. Joseph, Missouri, to Sacramento, California. Riders rode between 75 to 100 miles before handing the valuable *mochila*, or saddlebag, over to the next rider. Horses were said to have been changed every ten to fifteen miles. The delivery of Abraham Lincoln's inaugural address is said to be the fastest Pony Express run ever made. It took seven days, seventeen hours. The pony express ran from April 3, 1860 through October 1861.

Horses began to evolve in North America over 45 million years ago.

It's commonly known that the winged horse from Greek mythology is Pegasus. However, did you know that Pegasus was the son of Poseidon and Medusa, and when this mythological creature struck the earth with his powerful hoof, a spring appeared?

Long thought to have originated in Russia, the Akhal-Teke horse breed actually predates Russia and is believed to have come from the area now known as Turkmenistan. Known for its speed, stamina, comfortable gaits, intelligence, and ease in training, the Akhal-Teke have been given to heads of state as gifts over the years. The most noted gift was a stallion by the name of Melekush, given to Queen Elizabeth II by Nikita Khrushchev. The first Akhal-Teke stallion ever to stand for breeding in the United States was shipped to Virginia in 1978.

If you live in North Carolina and grow cotton, you may want to consider getting a horse because it is illegal to use an elephant to plow cotton fields.

In 1782, James Watt, a Scottish engineer, coined the term *horsepower* to describe a unit of power. His inspiration for this unit of measurement came from observing ponies pulling coal from mines.

The central figure of Norse mythology was Odin, the God of war. Odin's magical horse was Sleipnir. He had eight legs and was able to travel the earth, through the sky, and over water.

Although the unicorn has long been portrayed as a beautiful white horse with a long flowing mane and tail and a golden horn protruding from his forehead, the original mythological figure actually has a lion's tail, a billy goat's beard, and cloven hooves. Before the United Kingdom began issuing European Union passports, the British passport actually carried a drawing of a unicorn depicted in the original description.

Superstition in Lincolnshire, England, mandates that if you see a white dog, you should be quiet and not say a word until you spot a white horse—and then your luck will be restored.

The first horse, the prehistoric eohippus horse, was only about the size of a fox or an average dog. It had a humped back and had toes.

More than 2,300 years ago, the Greek soldier, essayist, and historian Xenophon showed an understanding of the mind of a horse in his belief regarding fear in horses. He recognized that to force the horse to face his fears using cruel methods only serves to increase his fear. He believed that when we add pain to the fear, it only makes the horse believe that the source of the pain is the fear. When a horse is frightened of something, use patience and kindness to help him overcome his fear.

A horse typically sleeps between two and three hours a day.

The word hippocampus comes from the Greek word hippokampos, which refers to a mythological sea monster with the head of a horse and the tail of a dolphin. Two areas of the human brain are named hippocampus because their curved shape resembles that of a seahorse. They can be found in the temporal lobe of the brain and are believed to play a large part in memory. Maybe this explains why most of us have horses "on the brain."

Embarr, Niamh's mythical horse from Irish mythology, was said to have the ability to run across the sea and land without ever touching the earth or water. The name Embarr means imagination.

The longest tail ever recorded on a horse was that of a Palomino by the name of Chinook. It measured a lengthy twenty-two feet long! The longest mane on a horse belonged to a mare in California by the name of Maude. It was a whopping eighteen feet long!

There are several horse breeds native to Japan. According to the Japan Equine Affairs Association, here are the native horse breeds that reside in Japan and approximately how many still remain today:

Misaki Horse	88
Tokara Horse	116
Miyako Horse	21
Hokkaido Washu Horse	2,928
Noma Horse	47
Kiso Horse	117
Taishu Horse	79
Yonagumi Horse	108
Total	**3,504**

If these numbers continue to decline, native horses could soon be extinct in that country.

> **"** The wind of heaven is that which blows between a horse's ears. **"**

—Arabian proverb

Dyaus Pita, the sky father in the Vedic religion, is said to take on two forms. The first is a red, thunder-bellowing bull, and the second is a black horse adorned with pearls, symbolizing the stars.

Skeletal remains of eohippus, one of the earliest horse ancestors, were found in 1931 by an expedition conducted by the California Institute of Technology. Based on that finding, it's estimated that the animal stood about thirteen inches and weighed only twelve pounds. The eohippus dates back more than 45 million years, which means horses have walked the earth longer than humans.

Wild and uncontrollable, the Mares of Diomedes were four creatures from Greek mythology. They were said to be breathtakingly beautiful, man-eating horses. As Hercules' eighth labor, he was sent to bring the mares back, which he was only able to do after feeding the mares their own master. This was said to have calmed the mares, which were then set free.

Epona, the Great Mare of Gaulish mythology, later appeared in Roman mythology as the protector of horses, donkeys, and mules. According to French historian, Benoit, she is also believed by some to accompany souls to the land of the dead. She is often depicted with foals by her side, indicating that she may have had some significance to fertility.

> "For want of a Nail, the Shoe was lost; for want of a Shoe the Horse was lost; and for want of a Horse, the Rider was lost; being overtaken and slain by the Enemy, all for want of Care about the Horse-shoe Nail."

—Benjamin Franklin, Poor Richard's Almanack, June 1758, The Complete Poor Richard Almanacks, facsimile ed., vol. 2, pp. 375, 377 (1970)

The Japanese believed that a spirit called Baku actually ate bad dreams. While descriptions vary, the Baku is said to have the head of an elephant, the mane of a lion, the body of a horse, the tail of an ox, and the legs and feet of a tiger. The symbol for Baku was sometimes even stitched onto pillows or pillowcases to ward off bad dreams.

ew people are aware of the wild horse population in the Waipi'o Valley region of Hawaii. Hawaiian state laws do not currently protect these horses, who are coming into increasing conflict with local farmers. According to Dr. William C "Billy" Bergin, large animal veterinarian, author, and animal care advocate, "These horses are a valuable and historic icon of Hawaii and need to be protected." The Humane Society and the Paniolo Preservation Society are hoping to eventually create a sanctuary for the horses. Dr. Bergin estimates that there are currently approximately thirty of these wild horses in the active farming area of the valley and believes that there is another herd of approximately thirty more on higher ground, at the convergence of two smaller valleys.

If you visit the island of Hydra, Greece, plan to travel by donkey, mule, or horse. Most other forms of ground transportation are banned.

" . . . through his mane and tail the high wind sings, fanning the hairs, who wave like feathered wings. **"**

—Shakespeare, *Venus and Adonis*

A horse uses more energy while lying down and rolling than he uses while standing.

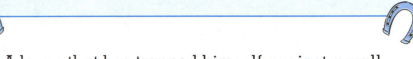

A horse that has trapped himself against a wall or other object and cannot stand on his own is said to be *cast*. Chances are he will find a way to free himself, but if he is in need of assistance, loop a rope over one or both of his far legs and pull. Be sure to remain calm and keep enough distance between yourself and the horse to prevent injury while the horse is attempting to stand. If you are helping a horse in a confined area such as a stall, once the horse is attempting to stand, leave the area to give him ample space.

Native Americans used to accustom their horses to being ridden (also known as *starting a horse*) by taking them into a pond or nearby lake. That first ride was often uneventful due to the fact that it was difficult for the horse to buck or rear against the pressure of the water. Once the horse settled down and accepted the rider, he or she would simply ride out of the water and begin the next lesson.

My horse has a hoof like a striped agate,

His fetlock is like a fine eagle plume,

His legs are like quick lightening.

My horse's body is like an

eagle-plumed arrow,

My horse has a tail like a

trailing black cloud.

—*Navajo song*

The term *zedonk* refers to an animal that is a cross between a zebra and a donkey. All horses, including zebras, belong to the genus *Equus*.

In Greek mythology, a centaur is a creature that is part human and part horse. Their descriptions vary widely. In some cases, they were believed to be wild, bad-natured creatures with animalistic behavior. In other depictions, they were kind, sensitive, and expressed a more vulnerable human side.

According to the Catholicism, the horse actually has nine patron saints: St. Giles; St. Vincent DePaul; St. Martin of Tours; St Anthony of Padua; St Coleman of Stockerau; St Eligius; St George; St. Hippolytus; and St. Leonard of Noblac. Since St. Frances of Assisi is the patron saint of animals, I suppose that would make it an even ten.

A way Out West

When placing or removing your Western hat, never do so by touching the brim. Oil and dirt from your fingertips will cause the edge to ripple. Always grasp your hat from the top of the crown. Never leave your Western hat in the sun as the color may easily fade. Instead, store it in a hat box in a cool, dry place between shows.

Try as you might to be present when your foal is born, most mares give birth during the nighttime hours. If you want to witness the miracle of birth, plan on sleeping with your boots on!

Horses are herd animals, which mean that most are not terribly fond of alone time. In an average herd, the mare decides when and where to go, and the stallion follows. See, horses are not really that different from humans!

Rearing and bucking are both undesirable behaviors in a horse and can injure the rider. The two main causes of rearing and bucking are pain and fear. Most horses do not intend to hurt you, so the key is to seek out the problem and solve it. Pain should be the first consideration. Inspect your tack, beginning with your saddle, and make sure that there are no particular spots that are rubbing. While the saddle is on, check the girth and the horse's belly to be sure the girth is laying flat and not pinching. Check your horse's teeth to rule out a sore tooth and look at the corners of his mouth to be sure the bit is not pinching. Once you have ruled out pain, pay attention to signs of fear, and then address each one. Once you eliminate pain and fear, you should have a horse that will be more willing to keep all four feet on the ground.

In order to ride every horse in the state of Wyoming, a cowboy had better get busy! It is estimated that there are approximately 5,000 head of wild horses still roaming around Wyoming.

The perfect Western pleasure riding position should create two simple lines. The horizontal line should consist of your horse's poll, withers, and hip, while the vertical line should be the rider's shoulder, hip, and heel.

Horses can sleep while standing up. This is possible because of the *stay apparatus*, a complex series of ligaments and tendons that stabilize the joints. The stay apparatus essentially locks a horse's legs into position, allowing her to remain standing while asleep. When you see a horse shift her weight to one side and close her eyes, there is a lot more going on than just sleep.

When clipping your Quarter Horse's bridle path for a show, lay his ear straight back as a guide to how far to clip the mane. Begin at the top of the mane and work down toward the withers.

n parts of Arizona, you will go to jail for as many as twenty-five years for cutting down a cactus, it is illegal to hunt camels, and you don't want to get caught riding your horse up the stairs of the county courthouse in Prescott.

According to the Bureau of Land Management, the wild horses that can be found grazing throughout the western United States are direct descendants of the horses that escaped (or were released by) early Spanish explorers, settlers, prospectors, Indian tribes, and the U.S. Calvary.

" It was in America that horses first roamed. A million years before the birth of man, they grazed the vast plains of wiry grass and crossed to other continents over bridges of rock soon severed by retreating ice. **"**

—Nicholas Evans, *The Horse Whisperer*

One of my favorite sayings is, talk to me of everyday things, and I am likely to ignore you; however, speak to me of horses, and you will have my full attention.

Over 100 years ago, there were approximately two million wild mustangs who roamed the open range of the United States. Today, that figure has dropped to an estimated 25,000 in the United States. They make their home in western states such as California, Idaho, Nevada, and Oregon.

In areas where sand is prevalent, a product containing psyllium is periodically given to horses to wash away any sand that has been digested while grazing. Psyllium is believed to help flush the sand through the digestive tract.

On some horses, you can find a dent on the neck or chest that's about the size of the tip of your thumb. Some Native Americans believed that horses carrying this dent were personally touched by God. They called this dent the *prophet's mark* and believed these horses were lucky. Whether or not he or she has a dent, I feel lucky just to be in the presence of a horse.

The North American Curly Horse has a coat with a texture that resembles a sheep, most likely the result of a dominant gene. The coat of a Curly Horse is reported to be hypoallergenic. Little facts are known as to the origin of the Curly Horse; however, ranchers in regions such as Nevada, the Dakotas, Colorado, Montana, and parts of Canada have been breeding them for decades. The curls on a Curly Horse can be found in the ears, on the whiskers, and even on the eyelashes!

The American Association of Equine Practitioners was founded in 1954 as a nonprofit organization and can easily be found on the grounds of the Kentucky Horse Park. Originally, the organization started with eleven veterinarians in the basement of the Brown Hotel in Louisville, Kentucky, but has grown to include over 8,000 veterinarians and veterinarian students representing fifty-seven countries; all of whom are dedicated to the health and welfare of the horse.

In Idaho, if you ever feel like you need to be in four places at once, just ride your horse to Heaven's Gate Lookout at Seven Devils Peaks. On a clear day, you will be able to look down into four different states at the same time!

66 If you're riding ahead of the herd, take a look back every now and then to make sure it's still there. 99

—Will Rogers

The gorgeous, spotted Appaloosa got its name from the Palouse region in Washington and Idaho states, in the area where the breed was first established. The name was first shortened to Appaloosey, (also spelled Apalousey) and then to the name Appaloosa that we know today. The breed has a rich history in the American West, and was even commented on in the journals of Meriwether Lewis, during the Lewis and Clark Expedition. There are approximately 677,000 of these beautiful horses registered with the Appaloosa Horse Club.

In Mexico, there is a type of rodeo called a *charreada*, which comes directly through history from Spanish horsemanship and the hacienda system. In *charreadas*, the cowboy is referred to as a *charro*. The women ride in an event called the *escaramuza*, which consists of eight women riding at top speed through a series of breathtaking maneuvers.

One of legendary gunslinger and outlaw Jesse James's horses was named Red Fox.

Outdated laws related to horses seem to abound. Here are just a few of the more humorous ones:

* If you're planning on going fishing while on horseback in Utah, put your poles away because it is illegal in some parts.
* In Culpeper, Virginia, it is illegal to bathe your mule on the sidewalk.
* In Wilbur, Washington, you can't ride an ugly horse.
* In Temple, Texas, it is perfectly acceptable to ride your horse through a saloon but never drive a horse and buggy through the town square.
* In Fountain Inn, South Carolina, all horses must wear pants.

When leading a horse, do not loop the rope around your hand. Instead, lay it across the palm of your hand before grasping it. If a horse bolts or spooks, this will limit your risk of injury.

The term *wall eye* refers to a horse that is lacking pigment in either one or both eyes. A horse's eye color and shape can vary from breed to breed and horse to horse. Black, brown, amber, and occasionally blue are normally occurring eye colors.

You break your nose, you break a window, you break a promise—all of which prove to be negative experiences—so why would you break a horse? A horse is simply *started* on a journey of a lifetime of learning. He is your partner, and once he is *broken*, you may never be able to fix him.

Streptococcus equi bacterium infections are commonly referred to as *strangles*, due to the fact that swallowing sometimes becomes so difficult that it can actually strangle the horse. If you suspect your horse has strangles, contact your veterinarian immediately. Strangles is extremely contagious from horse to horse. To prevent an outbreak in your barn, keep the infected horse isolated from other horses and sanitize everything that has come in contact with the infected horse.

There is a bone deep inside the human ear called the stirrup bone. It is so named because its shape resembles a stirrup, one of the many parts of a saddle.

Emmett Dalton, one of the infamous Dalton Gang, rode a horse named Red Buck. After receiving twenty-three gunshot wounds at the standoff that killed his brothers, Emmett served only fourteen years in prison in Lansing, Kansas, was paroled, and moved to California. There, he became a real estate agent, actor, and published author. He died at age 66.

Paint and pinto patterns are so incredibly unique that no two are ever identical.

A cluck to walk, a squeeze to trot, and a kiss to canter. Make your commands clear and concise in order to communicate exactly what you want from your horse.

The term *barn sour* refers to a horse that is uncomfortable outside of his existing environment. The barn sour horse will attempt to return to the barn or herd every chance he gets. It is an acquired trait that can be difficult to fix. To change your horse's attitude, allow your horse to be in sight of the herd or barn while leading or riding him for short periods of time outside his familiar surroundings. With each session, venture out farther and farther away, so that he realizes that he will eventually return to the barn. Remember that positive reinforcement is the key: You want to prove to the horse that spending time with you is just as desirable as standing in his stall or out in a pasture with his mates.

 The horse stopped with a jerk and the jerk fell off.

—Jim Culleton

Western boots have graced millions of feet, from the cowboys of the West to the pages of high-fashion magazines. Frye boots were worn by soldiers of both sides of the Civil War, soldiers in the Spanish-American, and by Teddy Roosevelt and his Rough Riders. There is a pair on display at the Smithsonian Institute, representing trends of the 1960s, but it would seem that the Western boot never goes out of style. Frye alone manufactures approximately 225,000 pairs every year!

A *remuda* refers to a herd of horses that are bred specifically to be used for ranch work. In 1992, the American Quarter Horse Association began rewarding ranches for their working herds with the Best Remuda Award. The award was created to recognize the contributions that ranch horses have made to the Quarter Horse breed, and it is considered a great honor to be recognized.

> " You can tell a gelding, ask a mare; but you must discuss it with a stallion. "
>
> —Unknown

Horses paw or strike the ground with their front hooves for several reasons. It can be to test a nice spot for rolling, to show their frustration for want of something such as food or attention, to warn another horse to back off, or to let you know that they are in pain.

In the state of Colorado, it is illegal in some cities to mistreat rats, for a man to kiss a woman while she is sleeping, to lend your vacuum cleaner to your neighbor, for car dealers to show cars on Sundays, to ride a horse while under the influence, and to bring your horse above the ground floor of any building.

Did you know that there are more than 150 internal parasites known to infect horses? Regular deworming, alongside good horse care, can help reduce or prevent many parasites. Intended for horse owners, www.myhorsematters.com is the official Web site of the American Association of Equine Practitioners. Their Web site offers the scoop on parasites, lots of valuable information on ways to prevent parasite infestations, and information on how to work with your veterinarian to create a deworming schedule that's right for your horse.

When introducing a new horse to an established herd, the herd's behavior should be watched closely. It is sometimes better to present the new horse by placing him in an adjoining pasture, either by himself or with one member of the herd, where he can be seen and smelled by the other horses until they are used to him.

The Galvayne groove, located on the corner of the incisor tooth in the upper jaw of a horse, can tell the age of the horse.

When the American Quarter Horse Association began registering horses, the number one was reserved for the stallion who won the title of Grand Champion at the 1941 Stock Show in Fort Worth, Texas. The horse to win the title was subsequently registered as Wimpy P-1.

The Wild Free-Roaming Horse and Burro Act of 1971 declared wild horses to be living symbols of historic significance and of the pioneer spirit of the West and placed them under the constant protection and management of the Secretary of the Interior.

Sports and Leisure

The Triple Crown is comprised of three races: the Kentucky Derby, the Preakness Stakes; and the Belmont Stakes. When the winning horse takes his place in the winner's circle, he is adorned with flowers—roses for the Kentucky Derby, black-eyed Susans for the Preakness Stakes, and white carnations for the Belmont Stakes.

For truly white socks on a horse the day of show, apply Bon Ami® cleanser by patting it on with your hand. (Baby powder works as well but tends to be too shiny.) Unlike other cleaning products, Bon Ami contains no ingredients that will harm your horse and can be found in the cleaning supply aisle in most grocery stores. As with any products used on your horse, always review the ingredients listed on the label to make sure they are safe and environmentally friendly.

Emirate Airlines is a major international sponsor of thoroughbred racing. In order to accommodate internationally transported equines, the airline's SkyCargo division has converted three A310F airplanes into air stables, which house horses in luxurious surroundings for the duration of the flight. (In-flight meals are included).

Since a horse is designed to run rather than jump, if given a choice, he will go around an obstacle rather than over it.

I was in awe as I spotted him in the early morning light of the Lexington, Kentucky, sun. As I walked over to the quiet, beautiful horse standing in the Living Legends section of the Kentucky Horse Park, I extended my hand in a gesture of friendship, and he tried to bite me! John Henry, almost 30 years old at the time, was a legend. He was the oldest horse to ever win the title of Horse of the Year at the ripe old age of 9, was the richest gelding of any breed in history, and was legendary for his bad disposition. It is said that the only time he was truly happy was when he was running.

Breeding season for horses in most areas is from February through June. Studies have shown a correlation between breeding and the length of days with sunlight. Did you know that you can extend this season by faking the length of days, using lights in the barn early in the morning and late in the day?

The heart of an average horse weighs approximately eight-and-a-half to nine pounds. Did you know that legendary racehorse Secretariat's heart was estimated at a whopping twenty-two pounds?

The ability to pick a good horse is truly a gift. In 1975, Karen and Mickey Taylor purchased a yearling for a mere $17,500. This gangly yearling was none other than the great Seattle Slew, who went on to win the Triple Crown in 1976!

The only horse to ever win against the legendary horse Man o' War was a horse named Upset.

———————————

Only eleven horses have ever won the elusive Triple Crown. They are Sir Barton, Gallant Fox, Omaha, War Admiral, Whirlaway, Count Fleet, Assault, Citation, Secretariat, Seattle Slew, and Affirmed. The last time a horse took the coveted title of Triple Crown winner was in 1978. The latest horse who was believed to have a chance to follow in the footsteps of these legends was a horse by the name of Barbaro in 2006. Barbaro was injured and never got his chance to take his place in Triple Crown history. When Seattle Slew died in 2002, it was the first time in Triple Crown history that there was not at least one past winner of the Triple Crown alive.

The word *tack* is used to describe the equipment necessary for riding a horse under saddle, while the word *harness* is used to describe the equipment used for driving a horse, such as with the use of a buggy or carriage.

It is believed that horses actually enter a REM, or rapid eye movement, stage of sleep, which is associated with dreaming. It is characterized by a deep sleep, in which eyes move from side to side under the eyelid, and various parts of the body twitch.

In cross-country jumping, the boundary flags are red and white. If the horse and rider do not jump between the two flags, they are considered out of bounds, and the team is disqualified.

During the Great Depression, if a man could find work at all, he earned an average of $500 a year. At a time when people needed a hero, one came along in the form of a small, crooked-legged racehorse who waddled like a duck. This horse began winning race after race while crowds cheered him on. This horse was nothing short of a miracle when a miracle was needed—and was none other than the grandson of Man o' War. This horse was the now-famous Seabiscuit.

In 2005, the Special Olympics hosted 16,914 athletes competing in equestrian events. Unified Sports is a program in which Special Olympic athletes compete alongside athletes without intellectual disabilities on sports teams for training and competition.

The mint julep is a combination of bourbon, mint, and sugar. Many claim that a mint julep, an outrageous hat, and a seat in the section that is referred to as Millionaires Row are the keys to having a great day at the Kentucky Derby.

Eclipse was a Thoroughbred who was named after an eclipse that occurred the year he was foaled. Eclipse is credited with the predominance of the Darley Arabian line in the Thoroughbred breed today.

According to The Jockey Club, the average cost for a Thoroughbred yearling race horse in 2005 was $13,500. This figure is substantially higher than the 1990 figure of $7,000.

Dr. Fager, a large stature, oddly proportioned race horse with two clubbed feet, had a total career winning figure of $1,002,642! He placed in twenty-one out of twenty-two races and was named Horse of the Year in 1968. People who knew him best did not remember Dr. Fager for his ability but rather for his sensitivity. He hated the jockey's whip and adopted a litter of baby kittens who were born in the corner of his stall. He was sad when the mother cat moved them! Dr. Fager set the mile record at the Washington Park Handicap that stood unbroken for an astounding twenty-nine years.

Secretariat won the Belmont in 1973 by a whopping thirty-one lengths!

The *gait* of a horse is a term used to describe how fast he is going. A horse's gait can go from a walk to a trot to a gallop or canter to a full run. Here is a great way to remember the gaits: Walking is for talking to the person next to you, the trot is a lot of bouncing and it's the second gait they do. The canter is for banter and it is guaranteed to make you smile, and a dead-out run is lots of fun to cover a quarter mile.

Julie Krone rode Colonial Affair at the Belmont Stakes race on June 5, 1993, becoming the first female jockey to win a Triple Crown race.

Citation was the first Thoroughbred to earn one $1 million in his racing career.

As soon as the winner becomes official at the Preakness Stakes race, a painter climbs a ladder to the top of a replica of the Old Clubhouse cupola and paints the colors of the silks to match that of the winning jockey. This tradition began in 1909 when a horse and rider weathervane sat atop of the Old Clubhouse. It was destroyed by a fire in 1966, and afterward, a replica was built.

Did you know that the Thoroughbred is the state horse of Maryland?

The movie *Dreamer* was very loosely based on a horse by the name of Mariah's Storm, who fractured her left front cannon bone in the Alcibiades Stakes race and went on to race again and win at Arlington Park, which now has a race named after her. She is the dam of several racing champions including Giant's Causeway, the 2000 Horse of the Year.

A horse by the name of Huaso holds the record for the highest jump at eight feet, one-and-a-quarter inches. He was ridden by Captain Alberto Larraguibel Morales in Santiago, Chile, on February 5, 1949. Just think: He could have easily jumped over Samson, history's tallest horse!

Ironically, Triple Crown legend Seattle Slew passed away on the twenty-fifth anniversary of the day he won the Kentucky Derby. He died peacefully in his sleep after siring 102 stakes winners, with earnings estimated at over 75 million dollars.

In 1938, when the two famous race horses, Seabiscuit and War Admiral, ran against each other, President Roosevelt kept a room full of advisors waiting so he could listen to the race. Seabiscuit gained more column inches of news-paper coverage than Hitler, Roosevelt, or any other public figure and won nearly sixty times his original sale price. War Admiral won the title of Horse of the Year in 1937.

Gymkhana events refers to timed speed events at a horse show. You may hear the announcer call the competitors by their entry number in this way: "Number 989, you're up; number 923, you're on deck; and number 546, you're in the hole." Being "up" means it is that horse's turn to compete, "on deck" means the horse will be next to compete, and "in the hole" means the horse will compete after the first two have finished.

According to the Smithsonian Institution's National Museum of American History, the famous race horse Lexington was actually buried in a coffin and placed in the ground in front of the barn that housed his broodmares. He was eventually moved and is currently in the museum's Behring Center.

Churchill Downs, the breathtaking site of the Kentucky Derby, is named after John and Henry Churchill, who originally provided the land for the park.

The record for the jockey with the highest percentage of wins belongs to jockey Isaac Burns Murphy (1860–1896). Murphy was an African-American jockey and is buried just steps away from the memorial statue of Man O' War at the Kentucky Horse Park in Lexington, Kentucky.

One quarter of a cup of coca soya oil poured over your horse's feed once a day will not only allow him to digest his food better, but will also result in a nice shiny coat.

The longest jump over water was really Something! Andre Ferreira rode the horse, who was actually named Something, in Johannesburg, South Africa, on April 25, 1975. The record they set was twenty-seven feet, six and three-quarters inches.

Dermatophilosis, commonly known as rain rot, is a bacterial infection of the skin. While advanced cases require veterinary attention, mild cases can often be treated at home by bathing the horse with an iodine shampoo. Prevention is easier than the cure. Keep your horses dry, well-groomed, and on a nutritious diet.

There have been recent changes in the Kentucky Derby. In 2004, a court order allowed jockeys to wear advertising logos on their clothing. In 2005, the purse was expanded to include the fifth place winner, not just the first four places.

For the year that their horse is the reigning Belmont champion, the winning owner keeps the Belmont trophy. The trophy is a Tiffany-made silver bowl with cover. The horse on the cover is none other than Fenian, the winner of the third Belmont Stakes, back in 1869. Three horses support the cup from below, and these horses are representations of the three foundation stallions of the Thoroughbred breed.

The Preakness was first televised in 1948, by CBS. Nearly 60 years earlier, George (Spider) Anderson became the first African American to win the race, taking home the victory in 1889.

The fastest horse on record was a horse named Big Racket, who was clocked at just over forty-three miles per hour.

Every year, only one horse wins the Preakness Stakes title. But in 1918, the race boasted a field of twenty-six horses, causing it to be run in two divisions, and the winner of each of the two divisions took home the title, thus making that the only year with two winners.

The Preakness Stakes, which is the second leg of the Triple Crown, is held on the third Saturday of May and is run by 3-year-old colts and fillies at Pimlico Race Course in Baltimore, Maryland. The original Woodlawn Vase, which is the trophy for the winner of the Preakness, now spends its days at the Baltimore Museum of Art and takes a field trip for race day only. It is presented to the winner on this day, and then returned to its rightful place until the following year. The winner takes home a smaller version of the actual trophy.

Man o' War was big, a full sixteen hands, and accordingly his farm name, or nickname, was Big Red.

One of the fastest American Paint Horses in history, Got Country Grip, won all of his first eleven races and is currently breaking records, including some of his own. He ran a remarkable race at Fair Meadows on June 9, 2006, breaking his own Paint Horse world record, with a time of 17.23 seconds for 350 yards.

The famous race horse Ruffian won every single race until July 6, 1975, when she broke her front right foreleg while racing Foolish Pleasure. She was laid to rest in the Belmont Park Race Track infield near the flagpole with her nose pointed toward the finish line.

The purpose of *longeing* your horse is to warm him up, stretch his muscles, and gain his attention. Keep longeing to a minimum, so you don't wear him out.

According to Jerry Bailey, former jockey and sports commentator, the most dangerous part of the race is actually the starting gate, due to close quarters and fear on the part of some horses. At most tracks, the gate is held closed by electricity until the start of the race. It takes approximately 5,000 to 6,000 pounds of pressure to trip a gate and open it before the start of the race. When a gate is opened prior to the official start of a race, it is referred to as a *false start*.

The average temperature of a human being is 98.6 degrees Fahrenheit; however, a horse's normal temperature ranges from 99.5 to 101 degrees. A fever in a stallion can alter his ability to reproduce for as much as 120 days. That is almost an entire breeding season!

A mentholated cold-relief rub, dabbed on the edge of your horse's nostrils, will mask other scents such as a mare showing signs of heat. If the horse is congested, the rub will also clear his airway and allow him to breathe easier, just as it does with humans.

If you laid out the long white fence that surrounds the 1,200 acres of the Kentucky Horse Park in Lexington, Kentucky, in a straight line, it would run for thirty miles! There have been horses on those 1,200 acres for over 200 years.

In 2004, a horse by the name of Smarty Jones won the Preakness Stakes by a record victory margin of eleven-and-a-half lengths.

The Three Chimneys farm in the Kentucky Bluegrass region has housed Thoroughbred legends such as Smarty Jones, Seattle Slew, and Silver Charm. In 1972, it started with 100 acres, three employees, and the dream of Robert Clay and his wife. Today, Three Chimneys has grown into a 1,500-acre farm with approximately 130 employees. The motto of this ranch has remained "Quality over Quantity."

Man o' War, arguably the greatest horse who ever lived, was born in 1917. He was sold at an auction in 1918 for $5,000, even though at that time, the average price for a yearling was closer to $1,000. Sam Riddle, who purchased Man o' War, certainly saw his potential.

The prestigious Belmont Stakes, the third leg of the Triple Crown, is held in June. It is for 3-year-old colts carrying a weight of 126 pounds and for fillies carrying a weight of 121 pounds.

It is believed that horses understand the tone of your voice rather than the meaning of your words. This must explain why my horses come running when I whistle.

" Horses stay the same from the day they are born until the day they die. They are only changed by the way people treat them. "

— "Silent Tom" Smith, trainer of the famous Seabiscuit

A grandson of Seattle Slew, Cigar, was a legend of racing. On a winning streak that lasted almost two years, he won sixteen races in a row, matching a record set by Citation. When Cigar retired, a retirement party was held for him in New York City. Fans gave a standing ovation and cheered as jockey Jerry Bailey rode Cigar for the last time.

In racing terms, a *length* is measured by the average length of a horse, and is approximately eight feet. Man o' War once won the Lawrence Realization race by a whopping 100 lengths! He also won the Belmont Stakes race by 20 lengths.

The first winner of the Kentucky Derby, Aristides, was trained by future Hall of Famer Ansel Williamson. The horse was ridden by African-American jockey Oliver Lewis.

The occurrence of twins in horses is unusual and can be dangerous to both the mare and the foals. Twinning is more prevalent in the Thoroughbred breed than in most others.

According to the American Paint Horse Association, horse racing has been a favorite American pastime for centuries. Although Paint Horse racing was first incorporated only in the mid 1960s, more than 600 starters competed in more than 800 APHA recognized races for purses of more than 5.1 million dollars in 2005.

War horses

It has been said that Julius Caesar rode a three-toed horse into battle. Although rare, this abnormality has been known to occur. Other historians have surmised that Caesar's horse was polydactyl. Descriptions of the horse vary from source to source, and depictions in art vary from piece to piece. Having unusual feet isn't the only feature that made this horse unique. According to legend, Caesar raised this horse with great care, because fortune tellers foretold that this horse would carry the future world ruler.

In parts of Kansas, legend has it that it is illegal to hunt whales, catch bullfrogs in a tomato patch, put ice cream onto cherry pie—and shops must provide a water trough for horses. Gaming regulations also prohibit the use of mules for duck hunting.

Cribbing is an activity in which a horse bites down on an object, such as a wall or feeder, and sucks air. It is believed to be caused by frustration, boredom, and by having excess energy from a high-calorie diet. This is an undesirable trait and can result in wearing down the teeth, digestive problems, or destruction of stalls and structures. It is much easier to prevent cribbing than to curb it. Make sure your horse's diet matches his energy requirements and that your horse has an enriched environment. If your horse must be in a stall for long periods of time, head off boredom by introducing toys or companion animals.

Teach a horse to fear you, and you might just over-come him, but teach a horse to respect you, and you will become one with him.

If your horse will not take medication in pill form, try crushing it up with a couple of strong mints. Honey or corn syrup work as well, but most horses love the smell and taste of peppermint.

In 1945, a group of Lipizzaner stallions was rescued and moved by train to escape the bombing of Vienna. Having been earlier separated from the stal-lions, the remaining group of mares and foals was stuck behind enemy lines in Czechoslovakia, which was in Nazi hands. General Patton sent his troops into enemy territory to bring these beautiful horses safely across the border.

In Fort Meyer, Virginia, a monument has been erected to a horse by the name of Black Jack. Black Jack was an army horse who became more famous not for who rode him, but rather for who did *not* ride him. Black Jack served as representation for our nation's loss by being the official riderless horse at funerals for servicemen and dignitaries. With the symbolic shiny black boots placed backward in his stirrups, he took part in the funeral procession of John F. Kennedy, Lyndon B. Johnson, and General Douglas MacArthur, just to name a few. Black Jack was the last horse issued to the Army by the Quartermaster and the last to carry the U.S. brand that Army horses wore. He died on February 6, 1976, at the age of 29.

Pain and fear are the two biggest motivators for bad behavior in horses. Their natural reaction to fear is to spook or flee and as with people, dealing with pain can cause a horse to act out.

When walking behind a horse, either walk far enough away that he cannot hurt you if he kicks, or walk closely enough that your body is touching his so he knows you're there.

A horse's hoof will grow approximately three eighths of an inch during one month's time, which means that it takes a horse approximately nine months to a year to grow a new hoof. The rate varies from horse to horse, and is affected by age, season, and nutrition, among other factors.

Hippophobia is not the fear of hippos but rather describes the fear of horses. *Equinophobia* is also defined as a fear of horses.

> **"** I can make a General in five minutes but a good horse is hard to replace. **"**

—Abraham Lincoln

Horses establish a sort of pecking order among the herd that decides which horse is the lead horse, or *alpha horse*. The alpha horse, generally a mare, is in control of the rest of the herd. The rest of the horses in the herd then follow her lead. Pecking order can quickly change when a new horse is introduced to the herd or by illness or removal of the alpha horse from the herd.

Heaves and inflammatory airway disease are two conditions that can affect your horse's breathing, but in conjunction with your veterinarian, you can help control the symptoms. If you notice any of the following symptoms, get your veterinarian to evaluate your horse's lung function:

* Cough
* Labored breathing
* Flaring nostrils at rest
* Increased movement of abdomen during respiration
* Elevated respiratory rate at rest
* Depression
* Nasal discharge
* Coughing up mucus and/or pus
* Exercise intolerance or poor performance

In Phoenix, Arizona, you had better check your spurs at the door because it is illegal for a cowboy to walk through the lobby of a hotel with his spurs on.

The sole survivor of the infamous Battle of Little Big Horn was none other than a horse named Comanche. He was purchased for a reported $90, and he was believed to be of Mustang descent. Comanche belonged to Captain Myles Keogh of the 7th Cavalry. Two days after the battle, the army found the fifteen-hand Bay horse severely wounded and transported him to Fort Lincoln, approximately 950 miles away. After a year of recuperation, he was excused from duty and remained with the 7th Cavalry. After living his life as a walking, grazing tribute to those who lost their lives at Little Big Horn, Comanche died of colic on November 7, 1891, at the age of 29.

The Royal Canadian Mounted Police, or "Canadian Mounties," are the national police service of Canada and an agency of the Ministry of Public Safety Canada. They first rode out in 1874 with only 310 horses.

Although the recommended daily allowance of water for humans is eight to ten glasses of water per day, a horse consumes an average of ten *gallons* on an average day! After a strenuous work session or a long ride, make sure your horse gets plenty to drink; however, do so in moderation by giving him small amounts at a time.

The Trojan horse, a well-known story from Greek mythology, recounts the end of the nearly decade-long siege of the city of Troy by the Greeks. The Greek army appeared to retreat, but the army left for the city of Troy a gift of a large, wooden horse. The city of Troy accepted the gift and brought the horse into the city, within the gated walls. That legendary horse was hollow and carried Greek warriors into the city unnoticed. These soldiers then opened the city for the rest of the Greek army, which had returned at night. This story is the origin of the phrase, "beware of Greeks bearing gifts."

Little Sorrel, the legendary horse owned by General Stonewall Jackson, was the horse that the general was riding when he was mortally wounded. Interestingly, the general is said to have been wounded by his own men! Little Sorrel was originally chosen for the general's wife.

West Nile virus is a relative newcomer to the United States. It is a disease spread by mosquitoes and can be deadly to your horse, so it's important that the West Nile virus vaccine be a part of your horse's vaccination regimen. The virus cannot, however, be spread from horse to horse or horse to human. This phenomenon is referred to as a *dead end host.*

A horse will lie down for a short time each day. When a horse that is perfectly healthy does lie down flat and outstretched, it tells you that he is comfortable with his surroundings.

In a canter or gallop, a horse will either be on a right lead or a left lead. The lead is noted by which front leg extends the farthest in front. Horses can switch leads without missing a beat, which is called a *flying lead change*. If the horse slows down to a trot in order to switch leads, it is referred to as a *simple lead change*.

The Andalusian horse originates from the Iberian horses of Spain and Portugal. The name is derived from the Spanish province of Andalucia. Once known as the perfect war horse, the Andalusian has carried men to battle, whether Romans or knights. The Andalusian is strong and solid and yet is elegant in movement. This horse is known for its breathtakingly beautiful mane and tail.

Horses can see extremely well. However, they do have two blind spots. The first is directly in front of them, and the second is directly behind them. When you reach out to touch a horse, approach her from the side and touch her neck. This way, you are in clear view.

If you watch horse's ears, they speak volumes about his mood. Be cautious when the ears are pinned to a horse's head. That is a sure sign that he is not very happy.

A horse spends almost its entire life standing up, so healthy hooves are essential to a healthy horse. Routine visits from your farrier, as well as keeping the hoof trimmed at the correct angle, are good ways to maintain a healthy hoof. Proper, professional hoof care can help prevent *laminitis* (also known as founder), an extremely painful and potentially life-threatening infection, and *white line disease*, a fungal infection that invades and separates the layers of the hoof wall. The protein in human fingernails is the same protein in a horse's hooves, and long fingernails and long hooves are more susceptible to bacteria than neatly trimmed ones. A horse's hooves should be trimmed every six to eight weeks.

" Nothing does as much for the insides of a man than the outsides of a horse. "

—Ronald Reagan

Not all horses grow *wolf teeth*, but if the sharp points of these teeth are present, they can cause pain, discomfort, or worse. Regular veterinary exams, starting as a foal, can help reverse or prevent many dental problems.

Although a horse is usually mounted from the left side, it is considered good practice to get him used to being mounted from both sides. In fact, it is a good idea to get a horse used to everything that you can possibly expose him to, because you never know the myriad of obstacles you may encounter.

In parts of Iowa, it is apparently a law that one-armed piano players must play for free, it is illegal to sell ice cream from an ice cream truck, a man cannot wink at a female he does not know, and horses are absolutely forbidden to eat fire hydrants!

All In the Family

On especially hot days, schedule your riding time in the early morning hours or late in the evening, when it is cooler. Keep a spray bottle of water in the refrigerator and mist your horse occasionally throughout the day.

A horse has approximately 205 bones.

Multitasking has become a way of life. When it's cold outside, watch a training video or a horse-themed movie while cleaning and organizing your tack. You accomplish two things at once, and you just may learn something new.

The top five ways to lose points in a Showmanship class:

- ★ Present a horse that is not clean.
- ★ Be late entering your class.
- ★ Perform the pattern incorrectly.
- ★ Forget your exhibitor number.
- ★ Touch your horse or the chain on the lead rope.

Be on time, be prepared, make eye contact with the judge, set your horse up quickly and efficiently, and show that you enjoy the class.

A run-through shed in a pasture can be an excellent alternative to keeping your horse in a stall. It offers shelter from the elements and provides your horse with plenty of fresh air and sunshine.

If you look closely at a horse's forehead, you will find swirls in the lay of his hair. The different patterns are believed by some to reflect the personality of the horse. These swirls are just one more trait that reminds us that no two horses are identical.

" Where in this wide world can a man find nobility without pride, friendship without envy or beauty without vanity? "

—Ronald Duncan, "Ode to the Horse"

Horses in the wild are naturally weaned at approximately 8 to 10 months old. Domesticated horses are weaned between 4 and 6 months of age.

althought a horseshoe is a symbol of good luck, many believe that if you hang the shoe upside down, all the luck will run out! I also suggest you remove the shoe from the horse before hanging it.

Layers are the secret to staying warm and toasty while riding during the winter months. The same holds true for your horse. A clipped horse will not grow a natural, thick coat that serves as a layer of warmth. Once blanketed in the fall, your horse should stay blanketed until spring. If you decide to blanket your horse, do so in layers and be diligent about keeping him warm all winter. Keep back-up blankets on hand to use while his regular blanket is being cleaned.

While there was once a long-standing debate about whether or not horses could see in color, most equine ophthalmologists now believe that horses do see in color, but in a way that's different from a human's perception of color. Horses only have receptors for two color bands, meaning that they likely perceive color in a way that is similar to how a person with red-green color blindness sees. Also, with far more receptors for light and dark, horses probably see in the dark far better than humans.

Horses are rarely bothered with fleas the way cats and dogs are. Fleas seem to have a natural aversion to the skin of a horse. Horses do, however, get ticks.

According to the National Hay Association and the United States Department of Agriculture, an estimated 150 million tons of hay is grown in the United States each year, making it the fourth largest crop per acreage, coming after soy, corn, and wheat. Of this amount of hay, approximately 71 million tons is comprised of alfalfa, with the remaining tonnage made up of assorted grasses and other hays. Within the continental United States, over 62 million acres is used each year for the production of hay.

> "On Easter, when you are sleeping, the Easter pony sneaks into your house and leaves you eggs and candy in your Easter basket."

—Explanation of the Easter bunny, as told by a 5 year old horse nut

For horses, winter brings many challenges. Frozen, hard ground and frozen water are two that are easily remedied. Keep either a run-in shed or stall bedded down heavily with sawdust, creating a nice, warm place for your horse to stretch out. Heaters for your water supplies are inexpensive, but be sure to keep the electrical cord out of reach, and always use a grounded plug to avoid electrocution.

You purchase health insurance and life insurance for yourself, so why not for your horse? There are insurance companies that specialize in equine insurance. There are also companies that specialize in equine appraisal that can tell you how much your horse is worth, in terms of an insurance claim, in case of an accident or injury.

Sheep and goats make excellent replacement companions for horses kept by themselves. Remember, though, that a horse is a horse, and nothing makes a better companion than another horse.

" Computers are like horses: Press the right button, and they will take you anywhere. "

—Unknown

Always store your feed in a cool, dry place, in a sealed container. A big barrel or a bin with a lid will keep feed dry and free of mold. The tight lid will also keep feed out of reach of the neighbor's dog, raccoons, mice, and other intruders looking for something to eat.

Although landscaping can be beautiful and can increase the value of your property, horse owners must be careful what they plant. Some popular landscaping choices can be harmful and even fatal to horses. Along with responsible pasture management, it's important to be aware of all of the ornamental plants that can poison your horse. Before bringing a new plant home, be sure to check with your local agricultural extension office to ensure that the plant you choose won't harm or kill your horse.

When bathing a horse, always start the spray of the hose at the horse's hooves and slowly move it up and over the entire body. Starting at the hooves will prevent the horse from being startled. For a mane and tail that are tangled and unmanageable, try using a leave-in conditioner or vegetable oil to loosen the tangles without tearing out the hair.

Routine trimming isn't the only way to prevent disorders of the hoof. Daily hoof care and cleanliness is also vital to maintaining a healthy foot. Did you know that a stone retained in the hoof can eventually work through the entire hoof and actually blow out through the hoof wall? It's true . . . and extremely painful for the horse. The use of a hoof pick to periodically clean out debris from around the frog, or center of the hoof, can prevent blowouts.

A garden leaf blower is an excellent way to clear the cobwebs from your barn. You can also use it to keep electrical outlets clean to avoid a fire hazard. In the spring and fall, a power washer is an excellent tool to keep your barn in tip-top shape, but never use it when temperatures are below freezing. Doing so can create a thin layer of ice, making even the most sure-footed horse or human slip and fall.

Just as with children, there are a variety of vaccines available for horses. Current offerings can help ward off West Nile virus; tetanus toxoid; Eastern, Western, and Venezuelan encephalomyelitis; influenza; rhinopneumonitis; strangles; rabies; Potomac horse fever; botulism; equine viral arteritis; and rotavirus A. Not every vaccination is appropriate for every region or every horse. Protect your horse by getting him vaccinated twice a year or on a regimen worked out with your veterinarian.

Observation can be the key to keeping your horse healthy. Spending time each day watching and grooming your horse can help you identify signs a problem early. For instance, a horse that frequently opens his mouth and rolls his tongue back and forth quite possibly has a dental problem. Frequent shaking of the head may indicate an ear infection, while eating dirt and manure may be a sign of a vitamin or mineral deficiency in the horses' diet. If you see behavior in your horse that is out of the ordinary, make note of it and always have your suspicions confirmed by a veterinarian before treatment.

Cold winter nights call for an extra-special treat for horses. A warm bran mash is like a warm bowl of oatmeal for any horse. To make a warm bran mash, in a bucket, mix:

1 cup bran
1 cup hot water
1 cup grain or oats
1 cup chopped apples or bananas
¼ cup of a dietary supplement intended for humans, containing psyllium. (psyllium is believed to help get rid of any sand your horse may have ingested in the pasture.)

It warms the horse and cleans the digestive tract.

The intestine of an adult horse is approximately ninety feet long!

When teaching your horse to load into a trailer, take your time and praise your horse for every step he takes toward loading. Be patient and show him there is nothing to fear. For a horse with extreme reluctance, try parking the trailer in an enclosed area with your horse and place his feed in the trailer. Hunger is a really good incentive, and once he loads and unloads into the trailer a few times to eat, he will become less reluctant to load for you when there's no food involved. When choosing a paint color for the inside of your trailer, keep in mind that a lighter color will give the appearance of a larger space and will ease feelings of claustrophobia.

If your horse is rubbing his tail against his stall door or a nearby tree, it is most likely time to worm your horse. While you are waiting for the wormer to do its job, we have found that pouring a little antiseptic mouthwash directly on the top of the tail immediately stops the rubbing.

Avon Skin So Soft, mixed with water in a spray bottle, is an excellent fly repellant for horses and humans alike. As with any other cosmetic product, be sure to test it on a small patch of skin before applying to your body, or your horse's body.

The simplest difference between a Halter class and a Showmanship class is that in Halter, *the horse* is being judged on overall conformation. In Showmanship, *you* are being judged on your ability to present and control your horse.

Speaking of horses (and we definitely are) did you know that it is the *male* seahorse that gets pregnant and delivers the babies? The seahorse is the only species that does this.

Chestnuts are the brown scab-like growths on the inner side of a horse's legs, near the knee or hock. They serve as fingerprints for a horse, as no two chestnuts are exactly alike. If you pinch a horse's chestnut, he will likely lift his leg for you. Chestnuts cause a horse little or no pain, but if you desire a neater appearance, you can peel off the outer layer. If chestnuts are allowed to grow too long, you'll want to have a farrier remove them, rather than peeling them yourself.

Due to old laws still on the record books, in Chicago, Illinois, it is illegal to fish in your pajamas, to take a French Poodle to the opera, and for women over 200 pounds to ride horses while wearing shorts.

A horse loves freedom, and the weariest old work horse will roll on the ground or break into a lumbering gallop when he is turned loose into the open.

—Gerald Raferty

Although many horses may be physically limber enough to sit down and scratch their own ears with their back hooves, rather like a dog, your horse will be grateful if you pitch in to help soothe the itch. Try grooming your horse or giving him a bath. If that doesn't do the trick, try bathing him with a shampoo designed specifically for horses with sensitive skin.

When hanging a hay bag inside a trailer or in a temporary stall, be sure to tie it high enough that your horse cannot get a leg hung up or tangled up in it.

The American Saddlebred horse ranges in size from fifteen to seventeen hands. It has a refined head with pointed, closely set, alert, and active ears, and a beautiful long neck. Saddlebreds can be found in all fifty states and Canada, with small numbers in several other countries as well. They were the first breed claimed by the commonwealth of Kentucky as its own.

About the Author

Tena Bastian is a former 4-H advisor, the mother of two daughters, and now a grandmother. She lives on a small ranch and kennel in Ohio with her family, seven horses, two dogs, and several cats. You can often find Tena and her husband Michael, or "Bear" as he is called by most, traveling the country presenting horse related seminars at major horse expos.

Known to many as a western poet, Tena is best known for her poem "Iron Horse." "Iron Horse" was seen in many major magazines including *EQUUS*, *Horse Illustrated*, and *Horse and Rider*. The original piece was auctioned at the All American Quarter Horse Congress and the proceeds were donated to the North American Riding for the Handicapped Association. Tena is the author of two previous books, *The Foal Is the Goal*, and *The Horses We Love, The Lessons We Learn*.

Tena strongly believes that a young life that includes the love of horses is a life that paves the way to a strong and confident adult. She's happy to share her love and knowledge of horses with all ages.